I WAS A baby DURING A Pandemic

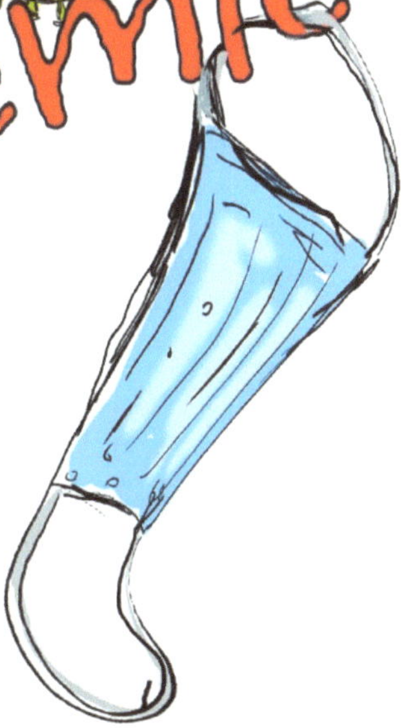

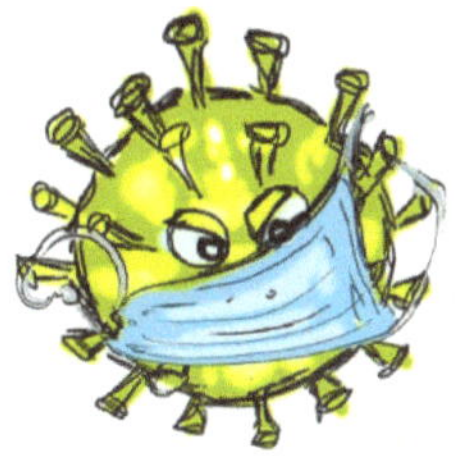

WRITTEN BY
GRACE MILLER

ILLUSTRATED BY
STACY JORDON

Vabella Publishing
P.O. Box 1052
Carrollton, Georgia 30112
www.vabella.com

Manufactured in the United States of America

ISBN 978-1-957479-47-7

Follow @storytellinggracefully for Author news and upcoming children's books.

To order books go to: www.storytellinggracefully.com

To my SONshine,
you are the brightest light
with a smile so contagious.
I love you baby of mine!

Hi! I'm Brodie.

I'm just a baby, but lately,
I've noticed a bunch
of strange things happening.

After the theme park we
visited closed early,
my family had to drive home...

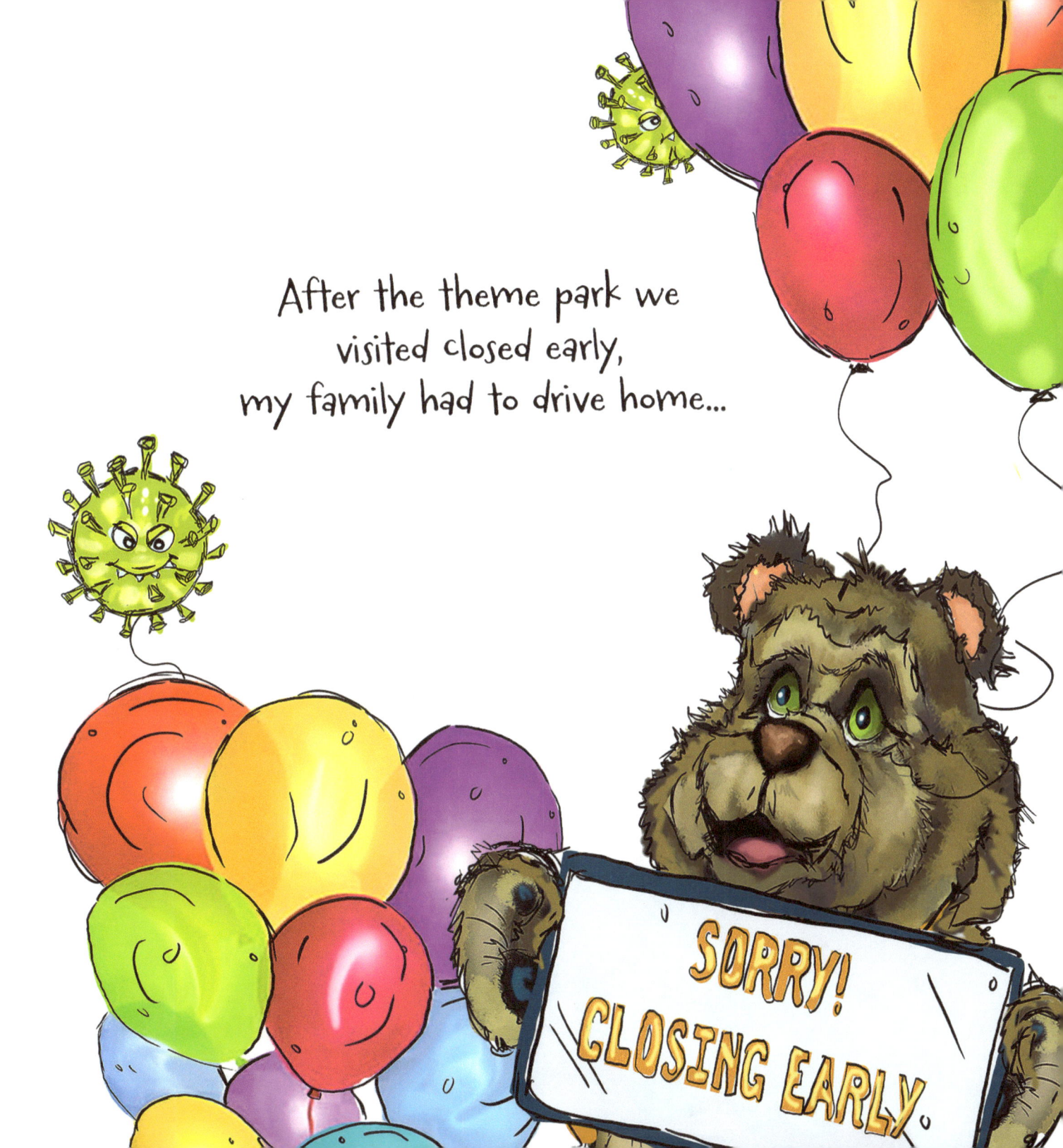

SORRY!
CLOSING EARLY.

When I started getting fussy in the car,
my Mama smiled at me.

I feel safe and comfortable when I see her happy face!

My Dad usually takes me to daycare on Mondays while Mama goes off to school since she's a teacher... but this Monday was different.

Today Mama said she was staying home to teach her students on the computer. Compared to our usual routine, this was quite different.

The next day, Dad carried me downstairs.
I saw Mama reading a book in front of her
computer. Her computer screen was filled
with happy children's faces, and the
sound of their joyful voices
made me smile.

We stayed home for a while after that,
and I started to miss visiting my
other family members and friends.
To cheer me up, Dad drove
me to the park most days.

Seeing my Dad make
silly faces at me in the mirror
makes me smile again.

When we eventually moved back out into the world, I noticed people standing far apart from each other.

"Stay 6 feet apart!" one worker shouted at the grocery store.

I was scared, but Mama made me feel better.

Her hugs make me smile whenever I feel frightened.

When I finally went back to daycare,
I noticed my teacher's smile
was hidden under a
mask of her own.

When I can't see her smile,
I feel scared.

Miss Kelly always plays fun music and dances with instruments, which makes me feel better.

When we went back outside, Mama took off her mask. I saw other people still wearing one, though... even while driving their cars!

I felt happy seeing
Mama's smile again.

Each day as Dad carries me into daycare, a small robot device floats in front of my forehead and makes a loud BEEP!

At school, my teacher still covered her face, but she continued singing songs and played games with me.

1 2 3 4 5 6 7 8 9 10

We made lots of bubbles during handwashing time! My teacher washed my hands more than usual and counted to 20 for some reason.

My classroom had fewer friends
this week, but
we still played and
laughed together.

I wondered when I would
see more smiles again,

but the most important
ones were at
home every day.

Even if there are masks covering your smile, you can find one. If you smile, you can change the world, but if you let the world change your smile, it will change your world as well.

So...Keep smiling!

About the Author

I'm a newly published children's book author with a passion for writing stories that offer different perspectives on relatable life topics. My love for writing began when I was a young girl who wrote in her diary every day. I began writing poems and fictional stories after receiving my first computer and eventually became an educator—teaching children ranging from preschoolers to middle schoolers—after graduating from college. My collective experiences as a student, teacher, and mother inspire me to write stories that both children and adults will enjoy, and my books aim to encourage readers of all ages to embrace empathy, kindness, and the power of a smile. I strive to find positivity even in the most challenging situations, with my stories reflecting this, and believe in the power of storytelling as a means to teach valuable life lessons while fostering personal growth.

About the Illustrator

Stacy Jordon has been an artist her entire life, finding inspiration in everything around her. Unlike specializing in one medium or subject, she fearlessly explores various techniques, creating diverse artwork that reflects her unique style. From realistic portraits to whimsical storybook illustrations, Stacy's art knows no bounds.

Her optimistic outlook on life shines through her art, celebrating the beauty and magic found in the world. Stacy's never-ending creativity leads her on an ongoing adventure of self-discovery, constantly seeking new ways to express herself artistically.

Embracing life to the fullest, Stacy feels incredibly blessed to share her journey. She illustrates children's books with her delightful vision and boundless imagination, captivating young hearts with a visual wonderland.

www.ArtbyStacyJ.com